100 facts
Whales & Dolphins

100 facts
Whales & Dolphins

Steve Parker

Consultant: Camilla de la Bedoyere

First published as hardback in 2006 by Miles Kelly Publishing Ltd
Harding's Barn, Bardfield End Green, Thaxted, Essex, CM6 3PX, UK

2 4 6 8 10 9 7 5 3 1

This edition printed 2010

Editorial Director: Belinda Gallagher
Art Director: Jo Brewer
Editor: Amanda Askew
Editorial Assistant: Carly Blake
Volume Designer: Elaine Wilkinson
Picture Researcher: Laura Faulder
Indexer: Jane Parker
Reprographics: Anthony Cambray, Stephan Davis,
Liberty Newton, Ian Paulyn
Production Manager: Elizabeth Brunwin
Editions Manager: Bethan Ellish

ISBN 978-1-84236-964-7

Printed in China

British Library Cataloguing-in-Publication Data
A catalogue record for this book is available from the British Library

ACKNOWLEDGEMENTS
Cover artwork by Mike Saunders

The publishers would like to thank the following
sources for the use of their photographs:
Page 41 Tui De Roy/Minden Pictures/FLPA; 45 www.pictorialpress.com

All other images from the Miles Kelly Archives

Every effort has been made to acknowledge the source and
copyright holder of each picture. Miles Kelly Publishing
apologises for any unintentional errors or omissions.

Made with paper from a sustainable forest

www.mileskelly.net
info@mileskelly.net

www.factsforprojects.com

Contents

Whales and dolphins are warm!

1 Welcome to the watery world of whales, dolphins, and porpoises. Just like humans, these unusual creatures breathe air and are warm blooded. This is because they belong to the mammal group. All whales, dolphins, and porpoises eat animal prey of some kind, rather than plant food. Almost all live in the sea, with just a few kinds of dolphin living in freshwater rivers and lakes. This amazing group of marine mammals also holds many records—the biggest animal in the world, the largest hunter, and some of the fastest, deepest-diving, and cleverest creatures ever to have lived.

▲ Many kinds of dolphin live in groups called schools. Common dolphins are colorful, with yellow or tan patches along their sides and dark "spectacles" around their eyes.

One of the earliest known whales, *Basilosaurus*, lived about 40 million years ago and was 66 feet in length.

The greatest animals

2 **Whales are the biggest kind of animal in the world today.** Some are longer and heavier than the largest trucks. They need a lot of muscle power and energy to move such large bodies. As they live in the ocean, the water helps to support their enormous bulk.

3 **The blue whale is the largest animal ever to have lived.** It can grow up to 98 feet in length, which is as long as seven cars placed end to end. It reaches up to 150 tons in weight—that's as heavy as 2,000 adults or 35 elephants.

4 **On land, bears and tigers are the biggest hunting animals.** However, the sperm whale is more than 100 times larger, and easily the biggest predator (active hunter) on Earth. It grows up to 66 feet in length and 50 tons in weight.

5

The animal with the largest mouth is also a whale, called the bowhead. Its whole body is 59 feet in length, and its mouth makes up almost one-third of this. If the bowhead whale opened its mouth wide, it could fit 20 people inside.

▼ The blue whale is a true giant, as large as a submarine. Yet it is also gentle and swims slowly, unless frightened or injured.

6

Whales breathe air, like humans. They must hold their breath as they dive underwater to feed. A few of them, such as the bottlenose whale, can stay underwater for more than one hour. Most humans have trouble holding their breath for even one minute!

FINDING THE WAY

Several animals find their way by listening to echoes of the sounds they make. Can you tell which of these do?

1. Bat
2. Tiger
3. Bird

Answer: 1. Bat

One big family

7 The mammal group of cetaceans is made up of about 80 kinds of whale, dolphin, and porpoise. The whale group is divided into two main types—baleen whales and toothed whales.

8 Baleen whales are the largest members of the cetacean group and are often called great whales. They catch food with long strips in their mouths called baleen or whalebone. One example is the sei whale, which is about 52 feet in length and can reach a weight of 25 tons.

▲ The sperm whale is the biggest toothed whale. It only seems to have teeth in its lower jaw because those in its upper jaw can barely be seen.

CREATE A DOLPHIN!

You will need:
paper   colored pens or pencils

Draw a dolphin outline and color it any pattern you wish. You can name it after its color, such as the pink-spotted dolphin. Or use your own name, like Amanda's dolphin.

9 Toothed whales catch prey with their sharp teeth. This subgroup includes sperm whales, beaked whales, and pilot whales. One example is the beluga, also known as the white whale. It lives in the cold waters of the Arctic and can grow up to 16 feet in length. It is one of the noisiest whales, making clicks, squeaks, and trills.

10 Another group is made up of beaked whales. These are medium-sized whales with long, beak-shaped mouths. There are about 20 kinds, but some are very rare and hardly ever seen. The shepherd's beaked whale, which is about 23 feet in length, has been seen fewer than 20 times.

◄ The finless porpoise, with its blunt "beak" and bulging forehead, is one of the smallest cetaceans at about 5 feet in length.

11 There are six species of porpoise. They are usually quite small, at 7 feet or less in length. They have blunter, more rounded heads than dolphins. The finless porpoise, as its name suggests, has a smooth back with no fin.

▲ The dusky dolphin is very inquisitive and likes to swim and leap near boats, perhaps in the hope of being fed.

12 There are more than 35 kinds of dolphin. Most of them are 7 to 10 feet in length. They are fast swimmers and can often be seen leaping above the waves. The dusky dolphin is one of the highest leapers, twisting and somersaulting before it splashes back into the sea.

Inside whales and dolphins

13 Whales, dolphins, and porpoises are mammals, like humans. They have the same parts inside their bodies as humans. These include bones to make up the skeleton, lots of muscles, a stomach to hold food, a heart to pump blood, and lungs to breathe air.

14 Most mammals have hair or fur, including humans. Whales, dolphins, and porpoises are unusual because they have smooth, hairless skin to help them slip easily through the water. Only a few hairs, mainly bristles, can be found around the eyes, nose, and mouth.

Skull

Upper jaw

Lower jaw

Flipper bone

Rib

▼ Blubber is the layer of fat underneath the skin of whales, dolphins, and porpoises. It is about five times thicker than the layer of fat beneath human skin.

Skin

Blubber

Muscle

Blood vessel

15 On land, fur keeps mammals warm in cold places. The sea can be cold, too. Cetaceans have a different way of keeping in their body heat. They have a thick layer of fat just under the skin called blubber. In large whales, the blubber can be more than 20 inches thick!

16

Cetaceans often have small animals growing inside their bodies called parasites, such as lice. Parasites aren't needed for survival—the whale or dolphin provides them with food. Some baleen whales have their heads covered with barnacles (shellfish), which normally grow on seaside rocks.

▲ Barnacles are a type of shellfish. They stick firmly to large whales and cannot be rubbed off!

Backbone (vertebra)

▲ The skeleton of a whale or dolphin, such as this killer whale, is made up of bones. There are no rear leg bones and no bones in the dorsal fin (on the back) or in the tail flukes.

I DON'T BELIEVE IT!

The sperm whale has the biggest brain in the world. It weighs about 18 pounds — that's over five times the size of a human brain. As far as scientists know, the sperm whale is not the cleverest animal.

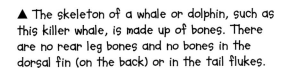

17

Compared to most animals, whales, dolphins, and porpoises have large brains for their size. Dolphins are clever creatures, able to learn tricks and solve simple puzzles. Some scientists believe that dolphins have even developed their own language.

Flippers, flukes, and fins

18 Most mammals have four legs and a tail. Whales, dolphins, and porpoises don't. They have flippers, a fin, and a tail. Flippers are their front limbs, similar to human arms. In fact, flipper bones and human arm and hand bones are alike. Flippers are mainly used for swimming, scratching, and waving to send messages to others in the group.

▼ The humpback whale waves its flippers in the air and splashes them onto the surface. This is called flipper-slapping.

19 The tail of a cetacean is in two almost identical parts. Each part is called a fluke. Unlike the flippers, flukes have no bones. They are used for swimming as the body arches powerfully to swish them up and down. They can also be slapped onto the water's surface to send messages to other whales. This is called lobtailing.

▼ Whales can often be seen splashing backwards into the water. This is known as breaching. Even the massive humpback whale can breach—and it weighs more than 30 tons!

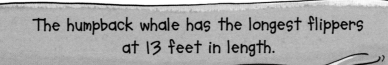
20

The fin on the back of many whales, dolphins and porpoises is known as a dorsal fin. In some, such as the killer whale, it is tall and narrow. In others, such as the bottlenose dolphin, it is shaped like a swept-back triangle. The blue whale has a tiny dorsal fin near its tail. Right whales, the bowhead, beluga, and narwhal have no dorsal fin at all.

MAKE A WHALE!

You will need:
long balloon   newspaper strips
paints   papier-mâché paste

Paste three layers of newspaper onto the balloon. Let it dry, then paint the whale and stick on paper fins and a tail.

21

Many whales, dolphins, and porpoises jump out of the water and crash back down with a big splash. This is called breaching. It may be done to send a loud message to others in the group, or to try and get rid of skin pests, such as barnacles and whale lice.

Sensitive senses

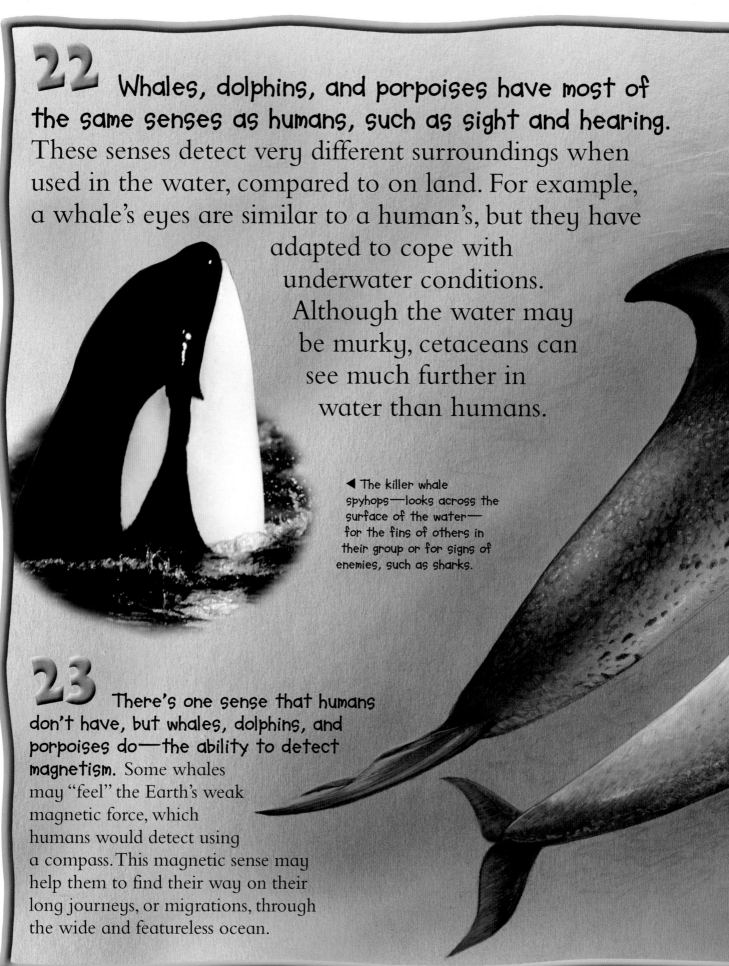

22 Whales, dolphins, and porpoises have most of the same senses as humans, such as sight and hearing. These senses detect very different surroundings when used in the water, compared to on land. For example, a whale's eyes are similar to a human's, but they have adapted to cope with underwater conditions. Although the water may be murky, cetaceans can see much further in water than humans.

◀ The killer whale spyhops—looks across the surface of the water—for the fins of others in their group or for signs of enemies, such as sharks.

23 There's one sense that humans don't have, but whales, dolphins, and porpoises do—the ability to detect magnetism. Some whales may "feel" the Earth's weak magnetic force, which humans would detect using a compass. This magnetic sense may help them to find their way on their long journeys, or migrations, through the wide and featureless ocean.

The fin whale makes a loud noise—it was once mistaken for the humming of machinery.

◀ Atlantic spotted dolphins roll over and rub each other. It's like saying, "Hello, we're in the same school."

24 Whales, dolphins, and porpoises have very sensitive skin, so the sense of touch is important to them. They rub and stroke others in their group, or a partner during breeding time. A mother whale often caresses her baby to provide comfort and warmth.

25 Cetaceans have a weak sense of smell, if any at all. Dolphins use their strong sense of taste to tell them about the foods they are eating. It also means that they can taste the water, too. This lets them know what other bits of food might be drifting nearby!

26 Hearing is vital for whales, dolphins, and porpoises. They don't have ear flaps or outer ears, like humans. Instead, sounds in the water are detected inside the head in the same way that the human inner ear works. Many toothed whales find their way in dark water by making clicking sounds, then listening to the echoes that bounce off nearby objects, such as rocks. This method is called echolocation.

Breathing and diving

27 **Whales, dolphins, and porpoises breathe air in and out of their lungs.** They don't have gills to breathe underwater, like a fish, so they must hold their breath when diving. Air goes in and out of their body through the blowholes—small openings on top of the head, just in front of the eyes. They work like human nostrils, just in a different place on the head!

▲ As a whale breathes out, its "blow" often looks like a steamy fountain of water. It can be seen far away across the ocean—and on a calm day, it can be heard from a distance, too.

28 **When a whale comes to the surface after a dive, it breathes out air hard and fast.** The moist air, mixed with slimy mucus from the whale's breathing passages, turns into water droplets. This makes the whale's breath look like a jet of steam or a fountain. It's called the "blow." All whales have "blows" of different size and shape. This can help humans to identify them when they are hidden underwater.

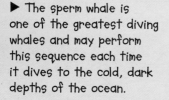

▶ The sperm whale is one of the greatest diving whales and may perform this sequence each time it dives to the cold, dark depths of the ocean.

1. The sperm whale surfaces and breathes in and out powerfully several times

2. It then straightens out its body and may disappear beneath the surface

▲ A giant squid tries to escape a sperm whale. The largest giant squid ever caught by a sperm whale was 39 feet in length.

29 **Many cetaceans feed near the surface, so do not need to dive more than 164 feet down.** The champion diver is the sperm whale. It can go down more than 10,000 feet to hunt its prey of giant squid.

30 **Most dolphins and porpoises dive and hold their breath for one or two minutes.** Large whales can stay underwater for a longer period of time, perhaps for 15 to 20 minutes. The sperm whale can dive for more than two hours!

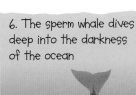
6. The sperm whale dives deep into the darkness of the ocean

3. The whale then reappears and begins to arch its back

4. By arching its back and tipping its head downward, the whale prepares to dive

5. Its tail is lifted out of the water as it begins to dive

Fierce hunters

31 **Dolphins, porpoises, and toothed whales are active hunting carnivores.** They eat meat—the flesh of sea creatures, especially fish and squid. Some of them crunch up hard-shelled crabs, shrimps and prawns, or shellfish, such as oysters and whelks.

32 **A typical dolphin has 60 to 100 teeth.** They are in pairs, left and right, in the upper and lower jaws. These teeth are not usually thin and sharp like fangs, but wide and cone-shaped. The teeth are the same shape all along the jaw, unlike the teeth of a cat, dog, or human. This is the best design for catching their slippery food.

33 **Beaked whales mainly eat squid.** In some species, males have just two or four teeth, which look like tusks. Females have none at all. These whales suck in their prey and swallow it whole.

34 **The sperm whale, has about 50 teeth in its lower jaw, which are about 8 inches long.** The teeth in its upper jaw are so tiny, they can barely be seen.

35 **Most dolphins and porpoises must chase their speedy prey, quickly twisting and turning in the water, snapping at victims.** Once a dolphin catches its prey, it flicks the fish back into its mouth, and swallows it whole. With a larger victim, the dolphin bites off a big chunk and swallows it. Whales, dolphins, and porpoises hardly ever chew their food.

▲ Bottlenose dolphins swim around small fish that gather into a tight group called a "bait–ball." Then the dolphins dash into the bait–ball and try to grab the fish.

21

Sieving the sea

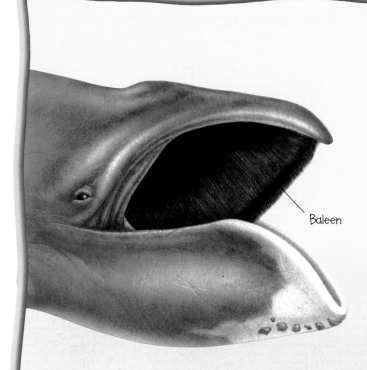

Baleen

▲ The bowhead whale's baleen hangs like a huge curtain, big enough for ten people to hide behind.

36 Great whales are also called baleen whales because of the baleen in their mouths. Baleen is sometimes called whalebone, but it is not bone. It's light, tough, and springy, almost like plastic. It hangs down in long strips from the whale's upper jaw. The size and shape of the strips vary from one kind of whale to another.

37 Most baleen whales, such as the blue, fin, and sei whales, cruise-feed. This means that they feed by swimming slowly through a swarm of shrimplike creatures called krill with their mouths open.

38 As a baleen whale feeds, it takes in a huge mouthful of water—enough to fill more than 100 bathtubs. This makes the skin around its throat expand like a balloon. The whale's food, such as krill, is in the water. The whale pushes the water out between the baleen plates. The baleen's bristles catch the krill like a giant filter. Then the whale licks off the krill and swallows them.

39 The humpback whale makes a "bubble curtain." It dives down, then swims up slowly in small circles as it breathes out. The bubbles created rise quickly and form a tube-shaped "curtain" that keeps the krill or other food close together in one place as a "bait-ball." Then the humpback lunges into the bait-ball with its mouth wide open.

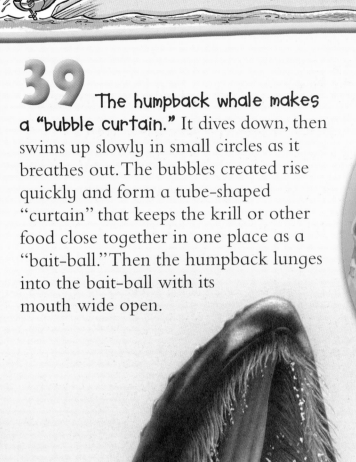

I DON'T BELIEVE IT!

In summer, the blue whale eats 4 tons of food in one day! That's about four million krill. In winter, it eats hardly anything for many weeks because food is scarce.

40 The gray whale often feeds on the shallow seabed. It swims on one side and drags its mouth through the mud. Then it pushes the water and mud out of its mouth. This traps food in its baleen, such as shellfish and shrimps. Its feeding method leaves deep grooves in the seabed, like a plowed field.

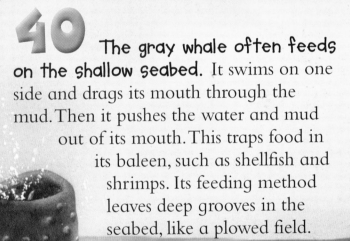

◄ Humpback whales feed by rising up through shoals of fish with their mouths open and throat skin bulging. They scoop up water, push it out through the baleen and eat the food left inside their mouths.

Clicks, squeaks, and squeals

41 **Many whales, dolphins, and porpoises are noisy animals.** They make lots of different sounds, for various reasons. These sounds can travel long distances through the sea, so when underwater, divers can hear them. Some whale noises can be heard more than 62 miles away!

42 **Sounds are made by air moving around inside the breathing passages, and also inside the intestines and stomach.** In dolphins, sound waves are brought together, or focused, by the large fluid-filled lump inside the forehead called the melon. This makes sounds travel out from the front of the head in a narrow beam.

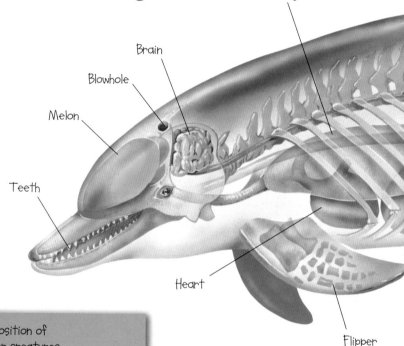

Lung

Brain

Blowhole

Melon

Teeth

Heart

Flipper

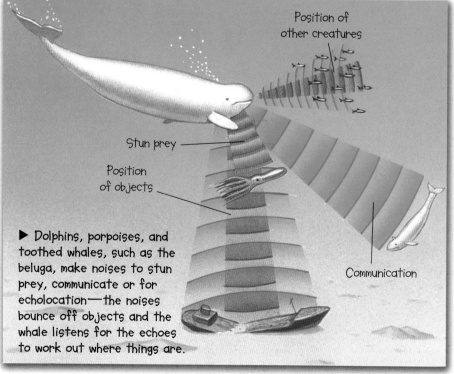

Position of other creatures

Stun prey

Position of objects

▶ Dolphins, porpoises, and toothed whales, such as the beluga, make noises to stun prey, communicate or for echolocation—the noises bounce off objects and the whale listens for the echoes to work out where things are.

Communication

43 **Sounds are especially important for detecting objects by echolocation.** The dolphin detects the returning echoes of its own clicks. It can then work out the size and shape of objects nearby—whether a rock, coral, a shipwreck, an iceberg, or a shoal of fish.

44 Sounds are also used for talking, or communication. Belugas and dolphins especially, make a vast range of clicks, squeals, and squeaks. Sounds help them to stay together in their groups, and to work together as they surround a shoal of fish.

Dorsal fin

Kidney

Stomach   Intestines

Liver

Bladder

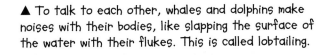

▲ To talk to each other, whales and dolphins make noises with their bodies, like slapping the surface of the water with their flukes. This is called lobtailing.

Fluke

◄ Most of the inner parts of a dolphin and a human are alike, such as lungs and heart. They are also in similar positions inside the body. However, a dolphin has no hip or leg bones—and humans don't have a sound-focusing melon!

MAKE SOME DOLPHIN NOISES

You will need:
sheet of card   ruler   plastic comb

Roll the card into a funnel and squeal through the narrow end. Rub the teeth of the comb along a ruler to produce dolphin-like clicks.

45 Scientists have spent time closely watching dolphins to try and discover if they use a language to communicate, in the way that humans talk with words. Certain sounds seem to occur more often when dolphins are resting, swimming, playing, feeding, or breeding.

Long-distance swimmers

46 Many cetaceans migrate—go on long journeys, usually at the same time each year. This is generally to find the best food. Baleen whales spend summer in cold northern or southern waters, where there are vast amounts of food. For winter, they swim back to the tropics, where there is little food, but the waters are warm and calm.

▲ Baleen whales, such as the humpback, travel long journeys so that they can give birth in tropical waters. Then the baby is able to grow stronger in calm waters before migrating to colder areas.

I DON'T BELIEVE IT!
The migration of the gray whale takes less than six weeks. It would take a strong swimmer 30 weeks to complete the same journey.

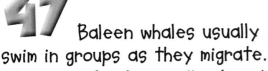
47 Baleen whales usually swim in groups as they migrate. They can often be seen "spyhopping." This means they swing around into an upright position, lift their heads above the water, and turn slowly to look all around as they sink back into the water. This is especially common in whales that migrate along coasts.

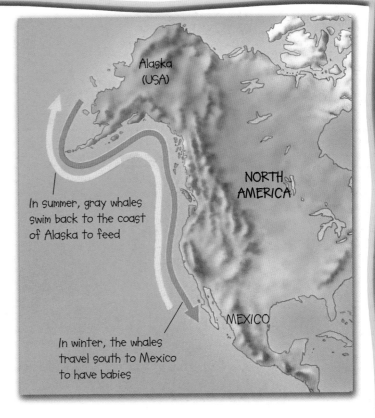

Alaska (USA)

NORTH AMERICA

In summer, gray whales swim back to the coast of Alaska to feed

In winter, the whales travel south to Mexico to have babies

MEXICO

▲ Gray whales travel up to 12,500 miles every year, between the icy Arctic region and warm subtropical waters.

48 The longest migration of any whale—and any mammal—is completed by the gray whale. In spring, gray whales swim from their breeding areas in the subtropical waters around the coast of Mexico. They head north along the west coast of North America to the Arctic Ocean for summer feeding. In the fall, they return in the opposite direction—a round trip of about 12,500 miles.

50 Many cetaceans can now be tracked by satellite. A radio beacon is fixed, usually to the dorsal fin, and its signals are picked up by satellites in space. This shows that some whales complete exactly the same migration every year, while others wander far more widely around the oceans.

49 Belugas and narwhals migrate from the cold waters of the southern area of the Arctic Ocean to the even icier waters further north! They follow the edge of the ice sheet as it shrinks and melts back each spring, then grows again each fall.

◄ A tracking beacon sends out radio signals to give a whale's position every few seconds or minutes. It only works when the whale is at the surface because radio waves don't travel far through water. The batteries can last for more than two years.

Family of killers

51 **All cetaceans are carnivores because they eat various kinds of animal as food.** The killer whale can kill and eat almost any creature in the sea, from a small fish to a large whale. It is also known as the orca and is not actually a whale, but the biggest member of the dolphin family.

52 Killer whales live in oceans all over the world. Their black-and-white markings make them easy to recognize. Males grow up to 30 feet in length and 10 tons in weight. They have tall, slim, triangular fins up to 7 feet in height. Females are slightly smaller and have lower, more rounded fins.

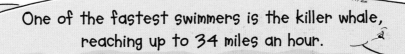

53 Killer whales live in groups called pods.

A pod is like a big family. Normally, there are 20 to 30 whales in a pod. Older females are usually in charge. Throughout the year, the females decide where to travel to, where to rest, and when the pod will hunt.

▼ A killer whale suddenly appears out of the surf and tries to grab an unsuspecting sea lion before it has time to escape.

MAKE AN ORCA POD!

You will need:
white card   scissors   sticky tape
black pen   cotton thread

Draw and cut out killer whales of different sizes. Thread cotton through a small hole in the fin of all but the biggest whale. Then, dangle each whale from the larger whale by taping them to its body.

54 Members of a killer whale pod talk, or communicate, by making noises, such as clicks and grunts.

They can then work together to surround a shoal of fish, such as tuna. The killer whale also feeds by "surfing" onto a beach and grabbing a young seal or sea lion. Then the whale wriggles back into the sea, holding its victim by its sharp, back-curved teeth.

Fast and sleek

55 **Dolphins are fast, active swimmers.** They always seem to be looking for things to do, food to eat, and friends to play with. They range in size from Commerson's dolphins, which are only 7 feet in length, to bottlenose dolphins, which are double the size at about 14 feet in length.

56 **Dolphins are often seen swimming with other dolphins in large groups.** Several kinds of dolphin sometimes form even bigger groups of many thousands. Pantropical spotted dolphins form huge groups and are very active—leaping and swimming. From a distance, the sea can look like it is boiling!

57 **Many dolphins like to bow-ride.** This means riding in the bow wave of a ship or boat—the v-shaped wave made by the boat's sharp front end slicing through the water. Exactly why they do this is not clear. They may be waiting for leftover food to be thrown from the boat. Or they may be saving energy by "surfing" in the ship's wave.

▲ The Pacific white-sided dolphin is about 7 feet in length. It can often be seen riding in the bow wave of small ships and boats.

► Dolphins, such as these bottlenose dolphins, can often be seen leaping out of the water together.

▼ When frightened, Fraser's dolphins swim close together with lots of low leaps and splashing.

58 Striped dolphins are some of the fastest swimmers. They live in all oceans, in groups of up to 3,000. Striped dolphins often jump clear of the water in long, low leaps as they swim at speed. This is called "porpoising," even when dolphins do it!

I DON'T BELIEVE IT!
The long tusklike tooth of the narwhal was once sold as the "real horn" of the mythical horse, the unicorn.

59 Spinner dolphins are well known for their spectacular leaps high into the air. Many dolphins somersault as they leap, but spinners twist and spin around as well, five or more times in each leap. They don't seem to mind if they land on their side, tail or head, and leap out to do it again.

River dolphins

▶ As the boto comes to the surface and breathes out, the noise it produces sounds like a human sighing. Its back has a low hump rather than a dorsal fin.

60 Several kinds of dolphin only live in rivers or lakes. Most are rare and face many risks. They include pollution, injury from the propellers of ships, and becoming trapped in fishing nets. Other dangers include being caught as food for humans, or starvation because humans have overfished rivers and lakes.

61 The boto, or Amazon River dolphin, lives in several rivers in South America. It has a very long, slim, beaklike mouth and grows to about 7 feet in length. It feeds mainly in the early morning and late evening. By day it rests floating on its side, waving one flipper in the air. When the Amazon rainforest floods in the wet season, the boto swims among the huge trees, along with giant otters and piranhas.

62 There are three kinds of river dolphin in Asia. One is the baiji, or Yangtze dolphin of China, which has a white underside and pale blue-gray back. The others are the Indus and Ganges River dolphins, which live in Indian rivers. They are gray-brown in color, grow to about 7 feet in length and are 176 pounds in weight.

63 Two kinds of dolphin live in both rivers and the sea, usually staying close to the shore. One is the tucuxi, which is quite small at just 5 feet in length. It can be found in the Amazon River and around the northeast coast of South America. The other is the Irrawaddy dolphin, found in the seas and rivers of Southeast Asia, from India to northern Australia. It has a blunt nose and blue-gray skin.

RIVER DOLPHINS

Can you match these river dolphins to the areas they can be found in?

1. Boto
2. Baiji
3. Indus River dolphin

A. China
B. Brazil
C. India

Answers:
1B, 2A, 3C

64 The franciscana or La Plata dolphin is a river dolphin that has gone back to the sea! It is similar to river dolphins, but lives in shallow water along the southeast coasts of South America. It can be recognized by its very long, slim, swordlike beak.

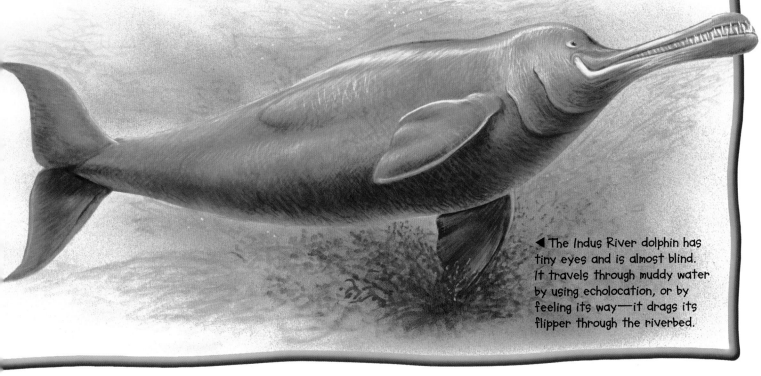

◄ The Indus River dolphin has tiny eyes and is almost blind. It travels through muddy water by using echolocation, or by feeling its way—it drags its flipper through the riverbed.

Shy and secretive

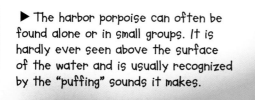

▶ The harbor porpoise can often be found alone or in small groups. It is hardly ever seen above the surface of the water and is usually recognized by the "puffing" sounds it makes.

65 **Porpoises are in a different subgroup to whales and dolphins.** There are six species, which are all found in the sea. Most live in shallow water near to coasts and shores. Like dolphins, they mainly eat fish and squid. There is one main difference between porpoises and dolphins—porpoises have spade-shaped teeth, whereas dolphins have cone-shaped teeth.

▼ The spectacled porpoise grows up to 7 feet in length and usually swims alone.

66 **The spectacled porpoise has a black ring, surrounded by a white ring, around each eye.** It can be found in the Southern Ocean around the lower tip of South America, and near islands such as the Falklands and South Georgia. It has a very striking pattern—its top half is black and its lower half is white!

67 The harbor or common porpoise is familiar to sailors around the northern waters. It has the nickname "puffing pig" because its blow is rarely seen, but can be heard as a series of loud, short puffs—like a mixture of a snort and a sneeze. It eats a wide range of food, including leftovers thrown from boats.

STRANDED!

You're at the beach and you see a stranded whale, do you...

A. Run away and keep quiet
B. Find an adult, and contact the police or coastguard
C. Sing the whale a song

Answer: B.

68 Dall's porpoise is the largest of the group, at about 7 feet in length and 440 pounds in weight. It lives along the shores of the North Pacific Ocean. It's a fast and agile swimmer, dashing along at over 31 miles an hour. However, it rarely leaps above the surface of the water like other porpoises.

▲ When Dall's porpoise swims quickly through water, a long, narrow spray spurts along its back. It is known as the "rooster's tail" due to its shape.

Getting together

69 Whales, dolphins, and porpoises breed like most other mammals. A male and female get together and mate. The female become pregnant and a baby develops inside her womb. The baby is born through her birth canal, which is a small opening near her tail.

70 Breeding narwhals can be dangerous. This is because the males swipe and jab each other with their long "tusks" to try and become partners for waiting females. The tusk is a very long left upper tooth that grows like a sword with a corkscrew pattern. Usually only the males have a tusk, which can be up to 10 feet in length.

◀ At breeding time male narwhals "fence" with their tusks. They're competing for a female.

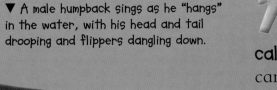

▼ A male humpback sings as he "hangs" in the water, with his head and tail drooping and flippers dangling down.

71 **When a male and female get together, it is called courtship.** They need to find a partner so they can have babies, otherwise they would eventually die out. For hours, they swim together and stroke each other with their flippers and flukes. They may also make noises, like "love songs." One of the most amazing is the song of the male humpback whale. He travels through the water making wails, squeals, and shrieks in a repeating pattern that lasts for up to 22 hours. Then after a pause, he does it again—just to attract a partner!

72 **Most cetacean mothers are pregnant for about 11 months.** When the baby is about one year old, the female can mate again. She can only have a baby every 2 to 3 years.

73 **Baleen whales have babies to fit in with their long journeys, or migrations.** They give birth in the tropics, when the water is warm all year. This gives the new baby time to grow and become stronger in warm, calm seas, before the migration to colder waters for summer feeding.

SWORDFIGHT

You will need:
straws   bucket of water
blue food dye

Put the food dye in the water. Hold a straw end in each hand, put your hands just under the surface, making the straws poke out above. Now start "fencing"—like two male narwhals having a swordfight.

Baby whales and dolphins

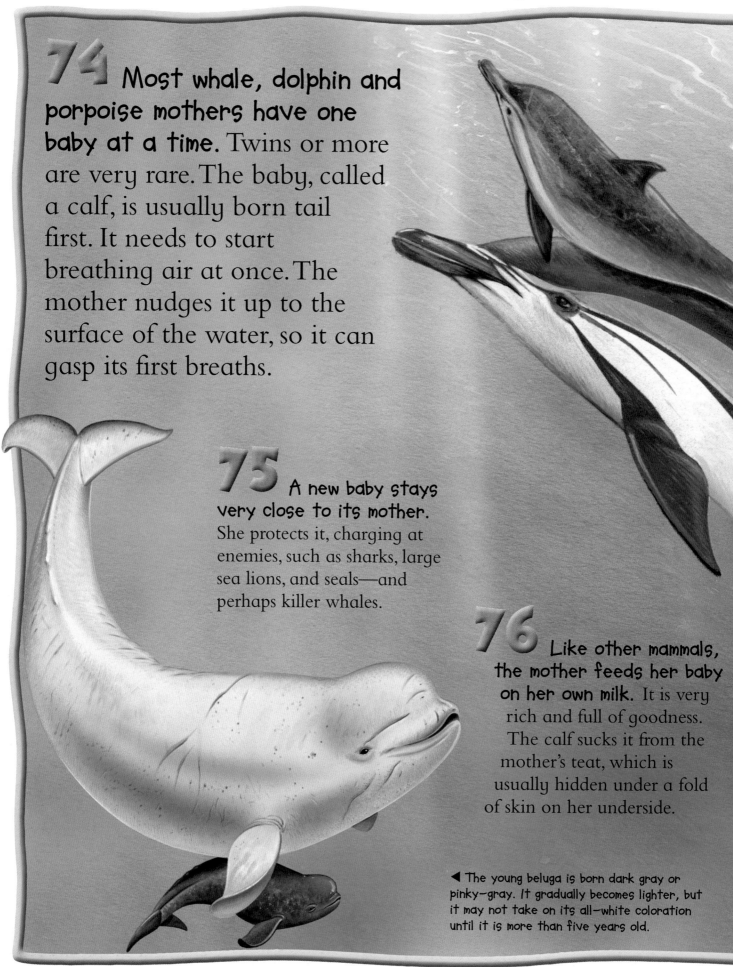

74 **Most whale, dolphin and porpoise mothers have one baby at a time.** Twins or more are very rare. The baby, called a calf, is usually born tail first. It needs to start breathing air at once. The mother nudges it up to the surface of the water, so it can gasp its first breaths.

75 **A new baby stays very close to its mother.** She protects it, charging at enemies, such as sharks, large sea lions, and seals—and perhaps killer whales.

76 **Like other mammals, the mother feeds her baby on her own milk.** It is very rich and full of goodness. The calf sucks it from the mother's teat, which is usually hidden under a fold of skin on her underside.

◄ The young beluga is born dark gray or pinky-gray. It gradually becomes lighter, but it may not take on its all–white coloration until it is more than five years old.

77 **Most baby cetaceans feed on their mother's milk for about one year.** They grow quickly and soon become strong swimmers. Their mothers teach them how to hunt. By 18 to 24 months of age, the young are independent—able to look after themselves. Baby baleen whales feed on their mother's milk for less time, for only 6 to 8 months.

I DON'T BELIEVE IT!
The blue whale is the world's biggest baby at 23 feet in length and 3 tons in weight. It drinks 92 gallons of its mother's milk everyday—enough to fill four bathtubs!

78 **It is difficult to know how long whales, dolphins, and porpoises live.** Scientists can guess their age from the way their teeth grow. Inside the teeth of some species are rings, like the rings in tree trunks. On average, there is one ring for each year of growth. Most dolphins survive for 15 to 25 years. Baleen whales may live for 70 to 80 years. However, some whales and dolphins have been known to survive much longer.

◀ Some baby whales and dolphins, such as this young striped dolphin, have different colors and patterns to the adults. Their colors change as they grow older.

Stories and mysteries

79 Thousands of years ago, the grace and beauty of cetaceans was greatly admired. The ancient Greeks and Minoans created pictures and statues of them in their palaces and temples, especially of common dolphins. Whale bones and carvings have been found in the remains of settlements that are 4,000 years old, from the Inuits of North America and the Norse people of Northern Europe.

▼ Common dolphins are pictured on the walls of the ancient palaces at Knossos in Crete, which were built by the Minoans about 4,000 years ago.

▼ The biblical account of Jonah says he was swallowed by a "big fish" or a whale. He is said to have lived inside it for three days and three nights.

80 Whales and dolphins feature in many songs, tales, and books. In the Bible, Jonah was swallowed by a whale. Rudyard Kipling wrote *How the Whale Got Its Throat*—it explains why the whale has grooves on its throat.

81 *Moby Dick*, written by Herman Melville, is one of the best-known whale stories. It is an adventure tale about Captain Ahab's quest to catch and kill a huge white sperm whale called Moby Dick because it had injured him.

82

One mystery about whales, dolphins, and porpoises is why they become stranded— washed up and stuck on the shore. Scientists have come up with possible reasons, but no one knows for sure. The animals may be ill, or may have been disturbed by storms or undersea earthquakes. They may be confused by local changes in the Earth's weak magnetism, which they could detect. Or they may simply be lost, looking for a way to escape predators.

▼ People may try to rescue stranded whales and dolphins, such as these pilot whales. It is a tricky task that needs skill and knowledge, and sometimes specialized equipment.

83

Most whales, dolphins, and porpoises are stranded now and again. Among the most common victims are pilot whales, also known as "blackfish." They live in close groups and have strong bonds with each other. If one whale strays too near the shore, it may become stranded. Other members of the group will often follow it because they don't want to leave the stranded whale alone. They then become stuck on the shore, too. Sometimes a group of more than 50 pilot whales ends up in a mass stranding.

The old days of whaling

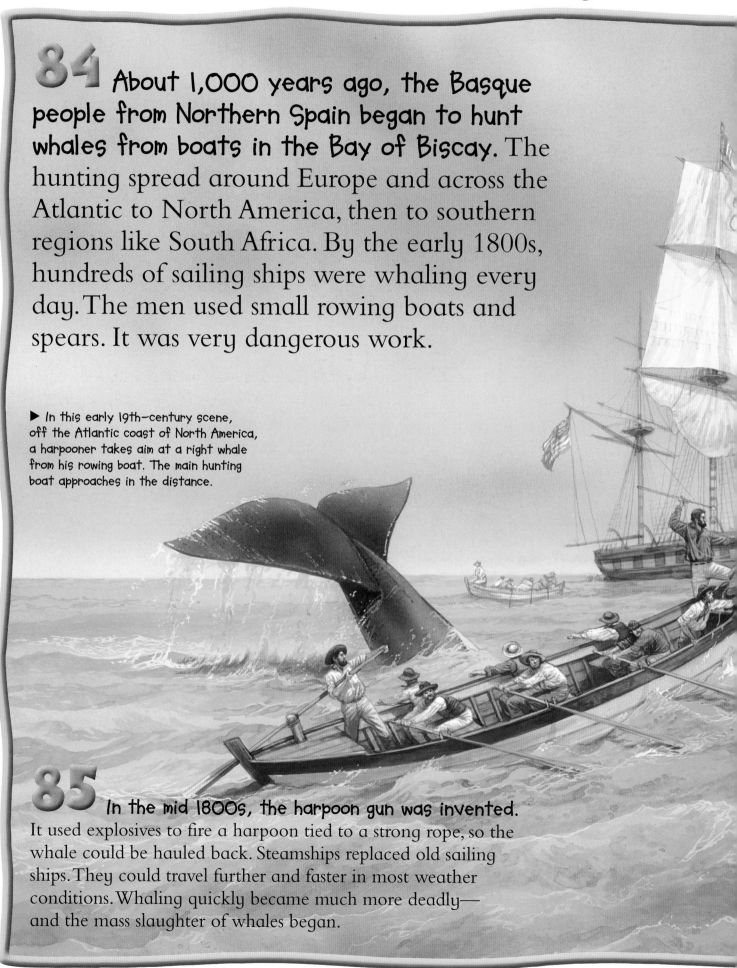

84 About 1,000 years ago, the Basque people from Northern Spain began to hunt whales from boats in the Bay of Biscay. The hunting spread around Europe and across the Atlantic to North America, then to southern regions like South Africa. By the early 1800s, hundreds of sailing ships were whaling every day. The men used small rowing boats and spears. It was very dangerous work.

▶ In this early 19th-century scene, off the Atlantic coast of North America, a harpooner takes aim at a right whale from his rowing boat. The main hunting boat approaches in the distance.

85 In the mid 1800s, the harpoon gun was invented. It used explosives to fire a harpoon tied to a strong rope, so the whale could be hauled back. Steamships replaced old sailing ships. They could travel further and faster in most weather conditions. Whaling quickly became much more deadly—and the mass slaughter of whales began.

Sailors once carved whale teeth, bones, and baleen into beautiful shapes, statues, and trinkets called "scrimshaw."

86

By the mid 1900s, whaling fleets were large and well equipped. Catcher boats pursued and harpooned the whales. Their bodies were hauled onto a giant factory ship for cutting up and processing. However by this time, many areas of the ocean had no whales left. They had all been killed.

87

Whales were used in many ways. Their fat, oil, and blubber went into foods such as margarines, and was burned in lamps. The meat was eaten in some areas, especially Eastern Asia. The baleen was used in machinery and for fashion items, such as women's corsets. Other body parts were put into pet food. The slippery substance called spermaceti, from the huge head of the sperm whale, was a high-quality lubricating oil.

88

During the 1970s, people around the world began to turn against whaling. It seemed cruel to spear and kill these mammals. Also, many kinds of whale were so rare, they were in danger of being killed off completely—extinction.

89

The International Whaling Commission controls the whaling industry. In 1986, it decided to ban mass slaughter of whales, with an international agreement, or moratorium.

90

Some whales have now returned to areas where they had been killed off. Whales breed slowly—females only have one baby every two or three years—so it will take a long time until whales are plentiful in the oceans again.

It's show time!

91 Many people visit an aquarium or sea-life center to see whales, dolphins, and porpoises. The most common cetacean kept in captivity is the bottlenose dolphin. Some centers have killer whales. A few even have minke whales. Although they are the smallest of the baleen group, they still grow up to 33 feet in length and 10 tons in weight.

92 Dolphins are clever creatures. They can learn many tricks, such as leaping through hoops, knocking balls with their beaks, and giving people rides on their backs. They can also recognize different shapes and count.

93 Dolphins can be interesting creatures to work with. Trainers are able to build a strong bond with them. Dolphins even change tricks or invent new puzzles to make them more fun.

▶ Bottlenose dolphins "clap" their flippers as if applauding, but of course, we cannot understand what they are really thinking.

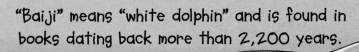

"Baiji" means "white dolphin" and is found in books dating back more than 2,200 years.

94

Some people believe dolphins should be set free to live in the sea. The dolphins are sometimes kept in small, bare tanks, with few toys to play with. They take part in several shows each day and can get bored and tired. They may suffer from loneliness or illness.

▶ The *Free Willy* movies told the tale of a boy's quest to set free a performing killer whale. In real life, the killer whale that starred in the films, called Keiko, was released into the sea near Norway.

WHAT A PERFORMANCE!

You will need:
thick card   scissors   pens or crayons
drinking straw   sticky tape

Draw, cut out and color a dolphin outline on card. Stick the straw to it, as a handle. Now invent tricks and put on our own show. Have fun!

95

There are arguments in favor of captive dolphins, too. If several dolphins have a big, safe pool, plenty of equipment and good food, they shouldn't get bored. Spectators can see what amazing animals they are, and hopefully learn more about saving wild dolphins and other sea life. Trainers and scientists can study the dolphins to find out more about them, for example, how they communicate, or talk.

Harm and help

▶ Pilot whales can be found in groups. This makes it easier for whale hunters to catch them.

I DON'T BELIEVE IT!
There are stories of people being saved by dolphins when in danger at sea. The dolphin may nudge them to shore. Some people even tell of dolphins protecting them from sharks!

96 Most baleen whales are protected by law around the world. Only a small amount of controlled hunting is allowed, although illegal hunting continues in some countries. Conservation parks, such as the Southern Sanctuary in Antarctica, are set aside to protect marine life.

97 However, hunting still goes on. Not only of large whales, but also of smaller whales, dolphins, and porpoises. Some whalers have turned to catching smaller types, such as melon-headed whales and pilot whales. If the hunting continues, they may also face extinction.

98 Whales and dolphins can drown even though they live in water. If they get stuck underwater for some reason, they cannot breathe and may die. One of the greatest dangers for cetaceans is becoming trapped in fishing nets—this causes nearly 1,000 to die each day.

99
Another hazard is pollution. Chemicals from coastal factories, power stations, and oil refineries wash along rivers into the sea. Some dolphins—especially river dolphins—and porpoises are badly affected because they live near the shore.

▼ Bottlenose dolphins soon learn to take food from divers, but this may affect their natural behavior and their ability to survive.

100
Ecotourism is becoming popular—seeing wildlife in its natural setting, while hardly disturbing it. People take trips on whale-watching boats, or swim with dolphins near the beach. The money made should be used to support wildlife and conservation. In some places this does not happen, and the whales and dolphins are disturbed or frightened. It's a delicate balance between our use of the sea and its creatures, and looking after their environment and well-being.

Index